PARIS
PHOTOGRAPHS 1935-1981
MAGNUM

Text by Irwin Shaw

With an Introduction by Inge Morath

An Aperture Book

Copyright © 1981 Magnum Photos, Inc., New York and Paris
Text copyright © 1981 Irwin Shaw
Library of Congress Card Catalogue No. 81-68200
Clothbound ISBN:0-89381-085-1   Paper ISBN: 0-89381-092-4
Staff for *Paris/Magnum:*
Magnum: Project Editor, Lee Jones;
Book Editor, Inge Morath; Associate Editor, Joan Liftin;
Associates, Tom Brazil, Ernest Lofblad, Sylvie Rebbot.
Aperture: Editor/Publisher, Michael E. Hoffman; Project Editor,
Carole Kismaric; Managing Editor, Lauren Shakely; Production
Manager, Stevan A. Baron; Designer, Wendy Byrne &
William Wondriska

Aperture, Inc., publishes a periodical, portfolios, and books to
communicate with serious photographers and creative people
everywhere. A complete catalogue will be mailed upon request.
Address: Millerton, New York 12546.
Manufactured in the United States of America.

Composition by Eastern Typesetting Co., Inc. South Windsor,
Connecticut; Printed by Acme Printing Company, Inc.
Medford, Massachusetts. Bound by Publishers Book Bindery,
Long Island City, New York.

Paris/Magnum accompanies an exhibition which opened in
November, 1981, at Musée du Luxembourg, Paris, under the
sponsorship of United Technologies Corporation. The
exhibition will travel throughout Europe and the United States.

This book is a double tribute.

It is a salute to one of the most talented groups in contemporary photography; and it is a fond evocation of one of the world's truly enchanting cities.

I hope you thoroughly enjoy Paris as it has been seen over the years by the men and women of Magnum. We are proud to have helped make the volume possible.

Harry J. Gray
Chairman and
Chief Executive Officer
United Technologies Corporation

MEETING MAGNUM

Inge Morath

When I first went to Paris to "meet Magnum" I went by train on the wooden benches of a third-class coach, with a new hat, a large number of sandwiches, and Ernst Haas, whose mother had brought the sandwiches to the Vienna railway station. The year was 1949. I had worked as an Austrian editor for *Heute* magazine in Munich and was trained as a writer and researcher. Ernst Haas was already a well-established photographer, and some of the stories we had done together had been brought to the attention of Robert Capa by the editor of *Heute*. Capa suggested that we come to Magnum in Paris and do some work, and we promptly did. Vienna still suffered from postwar restrictions; it seemed too small, and we were thirsting for the larger world. (Ernst Haas has taken extraordinary color pictures of Paris, but none in black and white, and thus is absent from this book.) Magnum Photos, the cooperative agency founded in 1947 by Robert Capa, George Rodger, Henri Cartier-Bresson, William Vandivert, and David Seymour, already had a big name. To have anything to do with this group was an exciting prospect.

Haasi and I got out at the Gare de l'Est. We can't have had much luggage, because in order to protect our small French funds we walked to the Magnum office at 125 Rue du Faubourg Saint-Honoré, which is quite a distance. The office was on the fourth floor. "The elevator," said a stern notice on the iron-grill door, "can be taken up but not down"—a piece of information we were already familiar with from Vienna, which must be the only other city that has such a restriction. We rang the bell, expecting all the big shots to come out to greet us. For a long time there was no response, but we went on ringing because we had had the arrival date confirmed in a letter. Finally, a tall thin man appeared with an icebag on his head. He was Carl Perutz, who photographed chic things brilliantly, and he had a hangover. "Today," he said, "is the Quatorze Juillet, Bastille Day, and I don't know if anyone will be coming to the office. But sit down anyway." He disappeared again.

The office was installed in an apartment in Maria Lehfeldt's name. (Her husband, Hans Lehfeldt, a great gynecologist, treated us all generously for bad backs, sprained ankles, and other such casualties.) The place still looked like an apartment, too, with a kitchen, bathroom, and bedroom. Only the big front room had a vaguely official air. Here were a long high table for editing, a phone on a long line that could be carried around, a few filing cabinets, and a couch on which I often slept when I had no money—a great convenience except for the absence of bed linen and the very early arrival each morning of the concierge to clean up.

On that first Magnum day of ours (there must be as many "my first day in Magnum" stories as there are "my first day in school" stories), Capa finally appeared in the company of his friend Len Spooner, editor of *Illustrated* magazine of London. Capa was handsome and full of life, and he made us feel right away that everything was under control, although so far nothing had happened. It did, soon enough: while continuing to plan Magnum projects with Spooner, Capa had picked up the phone, found us cheap hotel rooms, and firmed up a job for us with UNESCO in Italy. This done, we proceeded to Saint-Germain-des-Prés, where we had a glorious dinner. There were fireworks, the narrow streets were jammed with dancing couples, and Ernst and I showed everyone how to do the waltz-to-the-left. David Seymour, "Chim" to us all, turned up, too. He was gentle and more inclined than Capa to answer our myriad questions in detail. Cartier-Bresson, we heard, was at the time driving with his first wife, Eli, from the Orient to Egypt, and we would meet him later. George Rodger would soon arrive from Cyprus en route to Africa, and Werner Bischof would come from Switzerland en route to India.

The people who worked in the Magnum office were of various ages and specialities, but all were enthusiasts. Monsieur Ringard and Georges Ninaud and Madame Presle in files, administration, and accounting were older; editors varied in age, but I remember mostly young women, attractive and efficient, Hungarian like Capa and English and American; and there was a flow of researchers who were mostly Americans trying to make a living in Paris for a while. Lunch was often prepared in the apartment kitchen, although on more affluent days we would go to a small bistro around the corner. The café downstairs was the most important meeting place. There trips were planned and jobs were discussed and distributed, while Capa attacked the centrally positioned pinball machine.

Capa was the boss because, for one thing, he kept on the lookout for stories for all the Magnum photographers. But equally vital were his experience, generosity, connections, aggressiveness, and the vision he had for Magnum, which kept us going. Since few of us were married, we had much time to spend together. We talked a lot, but rarely about photography. Our discussions were more often about politics or philosophy or racehorses, pretty girls, and money. We constantly looked at each other's work, and criticism could be tough if the work did not measure up to the expected standard.

Paris was our base, a beloved city. We could get working permits and residence permits, live cheaply and as we pleased, slum it or go to the most chic parties as Capa's friends, or on our own, as our work began to open doors. Every so often, generous, nice people like Irwin Shaw, businessman Art Stanton, or film director Tola Litvak passed through Paris and invited a group of us to dinner at an expensive restaurant. We went to a lot of races at Longchamp. Bob Capa regularly got hot tips from

Robert Capa at the racetrack in Chantilly, 1952, by Henri Cartier-Bresson

Henri Cartier-Bresson by Jean Marquis

Group photograph at annual Magnum meeting in Paris, 1950s. *Front row:* Inge Bondi, John G. Morris, Barbara Miller, Cornell Capa, René Burri, Erich Lessing. *Between rows:* Michel Chevalier. *Back row:* Elliott Erwitt, Henri Cartier-Bresson, Erich Hartmann, Rosalina Bischof Burri, Inge Morath, Kryn Taconis, Ernst Haas, Brian Brake.

David "Chim" Seymour and Robert Capa by Henri Cartier-Bresson

the concierge at the Hotel Lancaster, and the rest of us also bet a little, putting our occasional winnings back into the brown Magnum kitty if it needed it. It usually did.

After marrying an Englishman, I moved to London in 1951. The sudden absence of photographers around me made me realize that what I really wanted to do was to take pictures myself. Until this time I had done research for Ernst Haas and other photographers and had written feature articles. Without telling anyone I began to photograph. After I had sold a number of my pictures and stories to various magazines, I returned to Paris and showed them to Capa. "O.K.," he said, "now you can join us as a photographer." I took any work I was offered. Since I was the greenhorn, mine were the smallest jobs. I started with a story for $100, about elderly gentlemen judging roses in the Parc de Bagatelle.

I also continued to do research for other photographers and to edit their contact sheets, an excellent visual training. I learned most from the contacts of Cartier-Bresson, who photographed with extraordinary economy and precision. He made me look at images upside down, the way painters do, to judge composition. Capa, who was quick to recognize the potential in people and to challenge them to bring it out by themselves, sent me on assignments that varied from photographing a movie set to shooting a story on a Spanish woman lawyer, to working as an assistant to Cartier-Bresson. Before sending me off to Spain he said that I should also work at getting myself dressed like a lady. I took his advice, and my reward was the look on his face when I showed up in my first Balenciaga. It was still a long time before I would move out of my one-and-a-half-room digs, where a gas stove stood conveniently next to the tiny bathtub (just big enough to sit in), so that I could cook breakfast while getting washed. There was no storage room, so my suitcases, covered with borrowed rugs, served as a second layer of flooring.

Those early Paris years of mine and of Magnum's lasted through the fifties. A picture agency wholly controlled and owned by its members (to my knowledge, the first of its kind), Magnum continued to grow. A steady flow of important photographic work took Magnum photographers all over the world. Battles were fought with newspapers and magazines over the right to approve the captions published with our photographs and to own our negatives instead of having to surrender them to the morgue of some big magazine. Group projects involving most of the photographers, especially those with *Holiday* and its great editor, Ted Patrick, were highly successful. Members included among others Eve Arnold, Erich Hartmann, Erich Lessing, Dennis Stock, Burt Glinn, Elliott Erwitt, Wayne Miller, René Burri, Bruce Davidson, Eugene Smith for awhile, and, in 1963, Charles Harbutt. As projects increased, so did the movement of photographers between Paris and New York. The world of magazines changed, just as the world itself was changing. In the sixties the scales tipped toward the Magnum office in New York, where industrial assignments and annual reports became increasingly important sources of income. The magazines were dying: *Collier's, The Saturday Evening Post,* and—incredibly— *Life* in 1972.

Magnum survives. Some old members left; new ones arrived, bringing with them new ideas and new visions. In sometimes stormy meetings, shifts in emphasis toward the more commercial or the more journalistic were endlessly discussed. Not much was ever reconciled, but it turned out that much could successfully coexist. Photographers are as individualistic as ever, and there are always great people on the staff (like the indispensable Allen Brown, who has seen it all since 1947). There may be less mothering now, but the need for a group sharing a concern for photographic excellence and integrity in work and personal conduct is as great as ever. The new generation carries on the tradition in Paris, too, from the office behind one of the great Parisian spots—the sensuous, delicious market in Rue de Seine.

On the evening of a late spring day in 1954 a group of us went down to the cafe under the Paris office to say goodbye to Robert Capa, who was about to leave for a project in the Far East. We had seen each other off to many places for many years, but somehow we were all sadder at this occasion. Capa worked hard on the pinball machine and mused about getting old—past forty. What would he do as an old man, he kept muttering? We all embraced in the dark, wet street, wishing "Bonne chance, mon vieux" to a man who had been brother and father to us all.

On May 25, 1954, Robert Capa was killed by a land mine in Vietnam. It was a stunning blow. Nobody wanted to believe it. Two days later a telegram reached us with the news that Werner Bischof had died in a car accident in the Peruvian Andes on May 16. The terrible sense of loss drew us closer together. Chim took over the presidency and Cornell Capa joined Magnum. Two years later, in the summer of 1956, gentle Chim was shot and killed in the Suez crisis.

We will never forget these three. They brought us together. Their totally different temperaments and ways of seeing and photographing expressed early on the variety of visions and the seriousness of work that has over the years been the distinction of Magnum. That they also loved to play and that they treasured friendship provided a communal warmth not usually found in photo agencies. To have chosen Paris as the place to begin it all was another stroke of genius of that wonderful mad Hungarian Capa, who talked Chim, Cartier-Bresson, and the others into working together in a cooperative named for a big bottle of champagne.

VIEWS OF PARIS, NOTES ON A PARISIAN

Irwin Shaw

My real appreciation of the problems and accomplishments of photographers developed during World War II, when I served in something called an Army Film Unit, which was deployed in Africa, England, and Europe. We were equipped with Bell and Howell 16-mm. motion picture cameras and our job was to record, as best we could, what went on in those theaters of war. The film we sent back was used by the newsreel companies, in propaganda and historic records produced by the army, and for storing in the archives. An argument in the unit that continued well into the war was whether or not a picture was worth a death. While the Army obviously considered it was, there was some difference of opinion in the ranks.

Among other photographers, in and out of the Army and several of whom were later to form Magnum, the question seems never to have been asked. Chief among these was the young man who was later to found and preside over Magnum, Robert Capa.

The photographs of Paris in this book, some of them Capa's, are all the work of men and women who pooled their varied efforts under the Magnum banner and who, like Capa, loved the city and expressed that love in a wide variety of images. The photographs speak for themselves, and I do not propose to interpret them or explain how they came to be created. There are many ways of looking at this superb collection: as high examples of the photographer's art, as a portrait of a great city, as a quirky probing of the characters and habits of its citizens at work, at play, at rest. My way of regarding this assembly is a particular one. I would like to see it as a generous tribute to the man who collected and was the guiding force behind the dazzling array of talents represented here.

I first met Bob Capa with a pretty girl in a bar in Greenwich Village. It was not the last time I was to meet him in a bar or with a pretty girl. Just returned from the war in Spain, which he had photographed with such brilliance, he was already famous, and I recognized him immediately: the thick-lashed dark eyes, poetic and streetwise, like the eyes of a Neapolitan urchin, the curled, sardonic mouth with the eternal cigarette plastered to the lower lip. Although he was famous, he was impoverished, a condition that, because of the hazards of his trade and his lust for gambling, was almost chronic with him. He was also in danger of being deported to his native Hungary, a country that he memorialized in his accent, a musical deformation of speech in all languages, which was dubbed "Capanese" by his friends.

Undaunted by his various problems, economic and governmental, and keeping hidden whatever psychic wounds his experience in Spain had inflicted upon him, he was gently and perceptively witty, with a gaiety that enchanted men and women alike. It was these qualities, along with a shrewd understanding of what people were like and a fearless ability to prove himself equal to all situations, that made him welcome at the headquarters of generals, in foxholes, at the best tables at "21" and the gaudiest of Hollywood parties, at the lowest bars in Paris and George's back room at the Ritz, at brawling poker games and fashion shows at the salons of the most modish Paris designers. He knew how to use his talents and his insights and if, as sometimes happened, you were exasperated with something he did and called it the old Hungarian charm, you did so knowing that if it pleased him he could turn it with good effect on you and you would fall for it, lend him the two hundred dollars he needed to replace the two hundred dollars you had lent him the night before and which he had promptly lost at the casino in Cannes. You would also forgive him for monopolizing your phone all day and bringing back girls from the beach who had not bothered to go home for a change of clothing and had to be properly covered in the morning with a wrap that you stole from your wife's wardrobe. He was not a proper guest or a proper friend or a proper anything—he was Capa and splendid and doomed and that was the end of it.

Now, what has that got to do with photography or anything? All. He was a free soul, at different times tormented and hilarious, and he roamed the world, as did his friends, outside ordinary considerations or conventions. Such men observe the truth and record it willy-nilly, and that is their value to us and themselves. That they contribute to the gift of their art the mechanical ability to bring things into focus and measure the duration of exposure of their lenses has nothing to do with their genius. Their insight, their touch, and their poetry is there—on the battlefield, in a quiet street, testifying to the general holy endurance of humanity.

Capa disposed of one of his problems—deportation—in a typical manner. At a party in New York shortly before the crucial day he announced that this was probably his farewell appearance, since the Department of Immigration had decided that as an alien without suitable papers he was due to be sent out of the country. One of the guests, a svelte and striking actress whom he had only met that evening, took him aside and offered to marry him immediately, thereby providing him with the opportunity of remaining in the country as the husband of an American citizen. Needless to say, Capa took advantage of this handsome offer, and, although the couple never lived together and eventually went through divorce proceedings, they remained friends until the end of his life.

In North Africa, where the army was faced with the necessity of fixing Capa's exact status, a command decision was made to consider him, with all necessary documents to prove it, a friendly enemy alien. Legitimized now, Capa made full use of his intuitive artist's eye, his instant grasp of the telling and significant moment, his coolness under fire, to reward the brass with a series of unforgettable photographs of our first campaign against the Germans, setting a standard that others might hope occasionally to reach but never to surpass.

For Americans at home their feeling of what the war looked and felt like in Africa was largely influenced by the work of this one man, and when the war shifted to Europe Capa was in the armada of gliders that was tragically mutilated by the fire from the ships of our own Navy standing off the coast of Sicily.

Whether this brush with disaster sobered him or not, his taste for being in the thick of things drove him into the long hell of Anzio and later, in London, inspired him to make five parachute jumps in one day to qualify him as an instant paratrooper, a skill that he was to utilize much later when he made the jump across the Rhine.

London before D-Day was a time of revelry for Capa, an occupation for which he had a highly developed taste. When he was not touring the pubs, he was the host at his girlfriend's apartment for intense poker games, during which, in the middle of the almost nightly bombings by the Luftwaffe, it was considered very bad form indeed to hesitate before placing a bet or to move away from the table, no matter how close the hits or how loud the anti-aircraft fire. If Capa was making money out of the war, the poker games made it certain that when peace came he would not be a rich man. He did not take losing to heart, though. When he came up with a pair against three of a kind or was caught with a four flush, the most he would say would be, "Je ne suis pas heureux," a favorite line from the opera *Pelléas et Mélisande* that he used on other, more dangerous occasions.

When D-Day came, with his uncanny sense for the crucial place at the crucial moment, Capa went in on Omaha Beach with the First Division. He was thought to have been killed, but turned up almost a day later in a hospital ship, with the precious rolls of film safely stowed away. The film was rushed to London for processing in the Time-Life office, where the boy who was to do the job was so excited by the magnitude of his responsibility that he bathed the negatives in hot water, thereby ruining many of the exposures, taken at such risk, and blurring the rest. When *Life* ran the redeemable photographs, the editors attempted to explain their hazy quality, to Capa's dismay, by claiming that in the heat of battle Capa had shot the film slightly out of focus. When Capa wrote a book about himself, he called it, bitterly, *Slightly Out of Focus.*

When I saw Capa at 12th Corps in Normandy, he said the experience had completely disillusioned him and that he no longer was much interested in photographing the war. Despite that, he covered the siege of Cherbourg and when we broke through at Saint-Lô, hitched rides with me in my jeep, happily recording on the way to Paris the freeing of large sections of France.

Naturally, he was in Paris on the day of its liberation, and some of the photographs in this collection show what he saw there. The shooting over, he looked up old friends from the time he had lived there before the war, among them a lady who had managed to hold on to the ownership of a bar on Rue Jean Mermoz and who embraced Capa tearily, as though he had risen from the dead, and then broke out a bottle of champagne to toast the reunion.

There are some people who are born to be Parisian and Capa was one of them. Worldly, handsome, languid, and dandyish when it suited him, ironic, mistrustful, on the best of terms with hotel concierges and the proprietors of small and excellent restaurants, he might have been born near the Bastille or in one of the great houses of the sixteenth arrondissement. Although the party in 1947 to celebrate the official founding of Magnum was given on Fifty-seventh Street in New York—and a wild party it was, a combination of a union meeting which had just unanimously voted to strike, a winning football team's locker room and a Roman Saturnalia—the headquarters and nerve center of the agency had to be in the heart of Paris. It turned out to be the famed cluttered apartment on Rue du Faubourg Saint-Honoré. In a small bar with a pinball machine conveniently located downstairs, the essential business was really conducted, deals made, photographers sent out to the far corners of the earth, acceptances and rejections decided.

Although he was now devoted to such peaceable occupations as signing contracts, arguing with editors, staving off creditors, and hand-holding nervous prima donnas, the outbreak of the first Arab-Israeli war found Capa once more under gunfire. He was on the beach in Tel Aviv when the radical wing of the Israeli army attempted to break the terms of a temporary truce by sending in an LST loaded with munitions, setting off a bitter fire fight between them and the soldiers of the ruling coalition, an action in which Capa, né André Friedman, was slightly wounded, leading him to remark, "That would be the final insult—being killed by the Jews!"

Later on, we were to do a piece on Israel together for *Holiday.* Capa was by now a local as well as international hero, and I found myself disregarded as the fellow who merely held the lights for the legendary photographer. When we tried to cross through the Mandelbaum Gate into the old city, held by the Arab Legion, we were halted by no less a personage than Major Tal, the military commander of the place, who spoke knowledgeably and approvingly of Capa's work, even though he regretted he could not let us enter his territory, since, he said, as Jews we would be torn apart by the frenzied inhabitants. I was ready to take him at his word, but Capa appealed to our vice consul, a man of traitorous disposition, and did everything but smuggle his way in as a Bedouin camel driver to get the shots he wanted. Happily, he failed, and the films we took back of the Great Mosque were made by an Arab photographer.

The work we did in Israel produced a book in which Capa's sympathetic talent for recording peacetime scenes and catching the character and mood of a people was displayed to good advantage. After Israel he swore that he was through with wars for good, and we were teamed together once more by Ted Patrick, editor of *Holiday,* to do a piece on Paris. In his photographs Capa made you understand why the city haunts every civilized man's imagination.

Patrick offered the job of picture editor for *Holiday* to Capa, which would certainly have improved his financial condition and probably kept him alive to a ripe old age, but Capa was already weary of the executive duties he had assumed at Magnum and opted to remain a working photographer. Also, while he loved America and Americans, he preferred living in Europe. Part of the reason for this might have been because the State Department, caught in the ugly tides of the McCarthy terror, was being disagreeable about his passport. I have always thought that it was to disprove the semi-official allegations that he was a Communist sympathizer that Capa accepted the job of covering the last days of the French war against the forces of Ho Chi Minh in Indochina.

I had made him promise not to get involved in any more wars, and when the news of his new assignment reached him, in Klosters, Switzerland, where we were skiing together, he merely told me that he was going to Japan for *Life.* When I asked him to bring back a camera for me, he glanced at me peculiarly, which should have warned me that he was not going to spend his time in the Orient photo-graphing the peaceful rehabilitation of the Japanese civilian population.

The last time I saw him was at the railroad station of Klosters, where he was serenaded by the town band as he climbed aboard the train with a bottle of champagne and someone else's wife.

Soon after, he was dead, blown up in an ambush eleven days before the war ended. Never a soldier, but with the soldier's prime virtue of always riding to the sound of guns, Capa received full military honors from the French after his death.

It was David Seymour, called "Chim," that gentle, scholarly, epicurean man, one of the founding members of Magnum, who called to tell me that Capa was dead. A few years later it was Cornell Capa, I believe, who called me to say that Chim had been killed in the Israeli-Egyptian war. My two friends had settled the question, each in his own time, about whether or not a picture was worth a death.

There is a healing magic about photographs. In a curious way they conquer time, or at least the time of your own life. Glancing at them you are once more strolling the sunlit streets that were familiar to you thirty years ago, and you are accompanied by glorious friends who were young then and had been through the war with you, laughing with them at private jokes, discussing their girls, arguing about politics or writers or reputations, making plans with them to go to the races or the Côte d'Azur or Deauville. Looking at their photographs, you see the city with their eyes, catch the temperament behind the shutter, lyric here, elegaic there, amused, happy, unhappy, but always vibrantly alive, always present.

For a few precious moments three decades vanish and memory, fleetingly, is blessed.

These are the members of Magnum, past and present, whose photographs appear in this book:

Eve Arnold
Bruno Barbey
Ian Berry
Werner Bischof
René Burri
Robert Capa
Henri Cartier-Bresson
Bruce Davidson
Raymond Depardon
Elliott Erwitt
Martine Franck
Leonard Freed
Paul Fusco
Jean Gaumy

Burt Glinn
Charles Harbutt
Erich Hartmann
Richard Kalvar
Josef Koudelka
Sergio Larrain
Guy Le Querrec
Erich Lessing
Constantine Manos
Inge Morath
Gilles Peress
Marc Riboud
David Seymour
Dennis Stock

PARIS
MAGNUM

Publication made possible by a grant from United Technologies Corporation

Henri Cartier-Bresson, 1952

Robert Capa, *25 août 1944*

Charles Harbutt, *Jardin du Luxembourg*, 1966

Elliott Erwitt, 1949

David Seymour, *Place de la Bastille*, 1952

René Burri, *Alberto Giacometti*, 1957

Elliott Erwitt, *Jardin des Tuileries*, 1969

Inge Morath, *Le Marais*, 1957

David Seymour, *Irène & Frédéric Joliot-Curie*, 1947

32 David Seymour, *Cirque Medrano*, 1935

Inge Morath, *Métro*, 1957

Inge Morath, *Rue Lepic, Montmartre*, 1957

David Seymour, *André Malraux*, 1936

36   Henri Cartier-Bresson, *Albert Camus*, 1952

Inge Morath, *Café, Les Halles*, 1955

Robert Capa, *Pablo Picasso, Rue des Grands-Augustins*, 1944

Robert Capa, *25 août 1944*

40   Marc Riboud, *Les Halles*, 1953

Marc Riboud, *Tour Eiffel*, 1954

Bruce Davidson, *Madame Fouché, Montmartre*, 1957

Bruce Davidson, *Montmartre*, 1957

45 Burt Glinn, *Françoise Sagan*, 1958

Robert Capa, *Café, Les Halles*, 1952

David Seymour, *Pigalle*, 1935

48   Guy Le Querrec, 1968

49   Paul Fusco, 1962

Inge Morath, *Bernard Buffet, Marie-Louise Bousquet*, 1957

Marc Riboud, *Rue Mouffetard*, 1959

Charles Harbutt, *Versailles*, 1978

Burt Glinn, *Crazy Horse Saloon*, 1956

56   Ian Berry, *Boulevard Saint-Michel*, 1963

Richard Kalvar, *Café, Le Marais*, 1965

58   Sergio Larrain, *Ile Saint-Louis*, 1959

Erich Lessing, 1957

Dennis Stock, *Café de Flore*, 1958

Werner Bischof, *Butte Montmartre*, 1950

Henri Cartier-Bresson, *Edith Piaf*, 1946

Jean Gaumy, *Paul Bocuse*, 1976

Marc Riboud, 1953

Elliott Erwitt, *Neuilly*, 1952

David Seymour, *Pablo Picasso*, 1937

69   Henri Cartier-Bresson, *Colette*, 1946

David Seymour, *Le Duc et la duchesse de Windsor*, 1952

Raymond Depardon, *Charles de Gaulle, Palais de l'Elysée*, 1967

Inge Morath, *Jean Cocteau*, 1958

Martine Franck, 1974

Henri Cartier-Bresson, *Place du Tertre, Montmartre*, 1955

René Burri, *Jean Tinguely*, 1972

Henri Cartier-Bresson, *Longchamp*, 1967

Bruno Barbey, *Saint-Germain-des-Prés*, 1968

Henri Cartier-Bresson, *Simone de Beauvoir*, 1946

David Seymour, *Front populaire*, 1935

Henri Cartier-Bresson, *Les Halles*, 1953

Dennis Stock, *Rue Jacob*, 1958

Sergio Larrain, *Champs Elysées*, 1959

Leonard Freed, *Rue de Seine*, 1974

Henri Cartier-Bresson, 1968

Josef Koudelka, 1981

Raymond Depardon, *Charles de Gaulle, Hôtel de Ville*, 1966

　　　Charles Harbutt, *Métro Bir-Hakeim*, 1973

Richard Kalvar, *Ile de la Cité*, 1975

Martine Franck, *Champs Elysées*, 1976

Martine Franck, *Etienne Martin*, 1967

93   Eve Arnold, 1977

94   Constantine Manos, 1965

Richard Kalvar, *Jardin du Luxembourg*, 1979

Charles Harbutt, *"Le Mistral,"* 1975

Bruce Davidson, *Jardin des Tuileries*, 1962

Inge Morath, *Janet Flanner*, 1973

Martine Franck, *Bois de Boulogne*, 1979

Charles Harbutt, *Rue Victor Schoelcher*, 1975

Gilles Peress, 1975

Bruce Davidson, 1962

Guy Le Querrec, *Concert Mayol*, 1979

Charles Harbutt, *Boulevard Montparnasse*, 1973

Leonard Freed, *Gare Montparnasse*, 1977

Josef Koudelka, *Musée du Louvre*, 1976

Guy Le Querrec, *Gare Montparnasse*, 1973

Charles Harbutt, 1973

Gilles Peress, *Métro Denfert-Rochereau*, 1976

Fabriqué et garanti par **bel**

The exhibition and publication
Paris/Magnum: Photographs 1935–1981
have been made possible by
United Technologies Corporation,
whose discerning support
reflects its concern for excellence
and its regard for the people
and culture of France.

Michael E. Hoffman
Editor/Publisher, Aperture

Lee Jones
Project Editor, Magnum